P9-DJU-617

Surrendering
OUR STRESS

PRAYERS TO CALM THE SOUL
AND STRENGTHEN THE SPIRIT

Joan Guntzelman

theWORD
among us®
press

Copyright © 2009 Joan Guntzelman

All rights reserved

Published by The Word Among Us Press
9639 Doctor Perry Road
Ijamsville, Maryland 21754
www.wau.org

13 12 11 10 09   3 4 5 6 7

ISBN: 978-1-59325-154-3

Unless otherwise noted, Scripture passages contained herein are from the New Revised Standard Version Bible: Catholic Edition, copyright © 1989, 1993 Division of Christian Education of the National Council of the Churches of Christ in the United States. All rights reserved. Used with permission.

Scripture passages cited as REB are taken from the Revised English Bible published by the Oxford University Press and the Cambridge University Press.

Scripture passages cited as NAB are taken from the New American Bible with Revised New Testament and Revised Psalms, © 1991, 1986, 1970, Confraternity of Christian Doctrine, Washington, D.C., and are used by permission of the copyright owner. All rights reserved. No part of the New American Bible may be reproduced in any form without permission in writing from the copyright owner.

Cover design by John Hamilton Design

No part of this publication may be reproduced, stored in a retrieval system, or transmitted in any form or by any means—electronic, mechanical, photocopy, recording, or any other, except for brief quotations in printed reviews—without the prior permission of the author and publisher.

Made and printed in the United States of America

Library of Congress Cataloging-in-Publication Data

Guntzelman, Joan, 1937-
Surrendering our stress : prayers to calm the soul and strengthen the spirit / Joan Guntzelman.
    p. cm.
ISBN 978-1-59325-154-3
1. Peace of mind--Religious aspects--Christianity--Prayers and devotions. 2. Stress (Psychology)--Religious aspects--Christianity--Prayers and devotions. I. Title.
BV4908.5.G86 2009
242'.4--dc22
                      2009018197

OTHER BOOKS BY JOAN GUNTZELMAN

God Knows You're Grieving:
Things to Do to Help You Through

Blessing Life's Losses

124 Prayers for Caregivers

Come, Healing God: Prayers During Illness

A Retreat with Mother Teresa and Damien of Molokai:
Caring for Those Who Suffer

In gratitude to my aunt,
Mary Pharo Meldon,
for her warm, loving influence for good
all through my life.

TABLE OF CONTENTS

Introduction / 8

1. Ask to Be Healed / 11
2. I Will Give You Rest / 12
3. Peace I Leave with You / 13
4. The Lord Will Guide You / 14
5. Give Thanks to the Lord / 15
6. Choose Love / 16
7. Wait in Silence for God / 17
8. Turn Fear into Trust / 18
9. God's Peace Surpasses Understanding/ 19
10. The Spirit Helps Us in Our Weakness / 20
11. Deliverance Is Nearer Than We Think / 21
12. Let Go of Distress / 22
13. Rescue Me, God, from My Troubles / 23
14. Fear No Evil / 24
15. Pray for One Another / 25
16. This Is the Day the Lord Has Made / 26
17. With Your Burden Go to God / 27
18. Live in Peace / 28
19. Change Is Possible / 29
20. Go to the Mountain of God / 30
21. The Lord Is Near / 31
22. God, Come Quickly to My Aid / 32
23. God's Spirit upon Us / 33
24. Become a Peacemaker / 34
25. The Gift of Challenges / 35
26. An Everlasting Love / 36
27. Give Thanks to the Lord / 37
28. Turn Mourning into Joy / 38
29. Let Gentleness Flourish / 39
30. The Lord Is with You / 40
31. God's Covenant of Peace / 41

32. In Your Trouble, Call to God / 42
33. Live Out God's Plan / 43
34. You Are Wonderfully Made / 44
35. Live in Love / 45
36. Turn to God / 46
37. Pursue a Foundation of Peace / 47
38. God's Angels Guard You / 48
39. Tell God What You Need / 49
40. Live with Joy / 50
41. Relieve My Troubles, O Lord / 51
42. Desire What God Wants / 52
43. Create Peace on Earth / 53
44. The Spirit Lives within You / 54
45. Receive God's Joy / 55
46. Welcome God's Wisdom / 56
47. Seek the Help You Need / 57
48. Withdraw into Peace / 58
49. Wrapped in God's Love / 59
50. Rejoice in God's Favor / 60
51. Let God Comfort You / 61
52. The Gift of Each Day / 62
53. Receive the Very Best of Gifts / 63
54. Give Thanks in Everything / 64
55. Do Not Let Your Hearts Be Troubled / 65
56. Encourage One Another / 66
57. God Hears Your Cries / 67
58. Trust in God's Gifts / 68
59. Be Present to the Lord / 69
60. Surrender in Prayer / 70
61. Breathe God's Love / 71
62. Be a Child in God's Arms / 72
63. Cast Your Burdens on the Lord! / 73
64. Turn to God Even in Your Anger / 74
65. Loosen the Bonds of Slavery / 75
66. The Power of Prayer / 76

67. Rejoice in God's Favor / 77

68. Pray Your Experiences / 78

69. Bear with One Another / 79

70. Do Not Be Afraid / 80

71. Rejoice in Your Gifts / 81

72. Cry Out to God / 82

73. The Intention to Do Good / 83

74. Hide in the Lord / 84

75. Claim Victory in the Lord / 85

76. Praise the Lord with Every Breath / 86

77. Discover God's Gifts in Life / 87

78. See with God's Eyes / 88

79. The Spirit Is at Work in You / 89

80. Cast Your Anxiety on God / 90

81. Choose Christ's Peace / 91

82. Faithful Friends Are a Gift of God / 92

83. Love Banishes Fear / 93

84. Let the Shining Face of God Warm You / 94

85. Come Away and Rest a While / 95

86. Be Strong and Courageous / 96

87. Let God's Love Be Your Comfort / 97

88. Give the Gift of Peace / 98

89. Welcome God's Care / 99

90. Love without Exception / 100

91. All Things Work Together for Good / 101

92. Be Peaceful and Gentle / 102

93. Peace Be to You / 103

94. Let Silence Speak Peace / 104

95. Return a Blessing / 105

96. Agree with God / 106

97. Rejoice in God's Presence / 107

98. Find God Within / 108

99. Be Clothed in Faith and Peace / 109

100. Don't Worry about Tomorrow / 110

Introduction

Life on this earth has always been stressful. Threats to our survival and well-being, whether from the natural world or from what we may perceive as dangerous, have been part of every age. In such situations, our innate response mechanism is triggered and set into motion. Our stress response is a healthy, inborn ability that supplies what we need to help us cope with the threats in our lives. We get into trouble, however, when the number or size of these threats overwhelms our ability to cope with them, or when our response is prolonged or inadequate for the task.

Today we live in a world that has multiple sources of stress. Whereas our ancestors found most of their threats to be directed at their very survival, in this modern age many psychological situations and beliefs also act as stressors in our lives. What we perceive as threats is unique to each one of us: while the identical situation may be defined by one person as highly stressful, another person may see it as an exciting challenge.

Stress has been described as the potential source of many physical and emotional illnesses and diseases. We see it playing a role in our relationships and job experiences. We also find ourselves distracted and disturbed in our spiritual lives by the multiplicity of stresses and worries we carry. Peace, the antithesis of stress, was a common theme of Jesus in his interactions with those around him. Many times he spoke of peace in terms of the blessing that it carries for us.

In our faith journeys, prayer and spiritual reflection can offer us wonderful opportunities to manage our stresses and work through them. Drawing close to God in prayer and Scripture can allow us to examine and consider our own lives and identify the stressors or our reactions to them. Being able to articulate and name what our problems are, and what our reactions tend to be, can help us find the peace we crave. We may discover that we have tendencies to overreact to certain situations, or to not give enough attention to the problems we do have. Perhaps we see a threat where none exists. Increasing our awareness of the role of stress in our own lives, and praying through our struggles with stress, may help us find the peace we seek and also help us to live more healthy and blessed lives.

Surrendering Our Stress: Prayers to Calm the Soul and Strengthen the Spirit is meant to help us examine our own lives and discern how we may be stumbling blocks to ourselves, even when we are not aware of it. We may be surprised when we discern what our own sources of stress are. As we become more conscious of them, we may find our reactions and ways of coping to be helpful in some situations and not so helpful in others. We may find new ways of managing our stresses that we hadn't considered before, and we may find prayer time to be a wonderful way of growing through the struggles of our lives.

The short reflections in this book can be used anytime or anywhere. They begin with a verse or two of Scripture, move into a short meditation, and end with a prayer. The prayer is meant to launch us into our own conversation with the Lord. However, if we are feeling particularly stressed, it may be the only prayer we are capable of at that moment. The important thing is that we are turning to God, who is our lover, our rock, our fortress, and our deliverer in times of trouble. To whom else shall we go for love, security and peace?

Joan Guntzelman

Ask to Be Healed

He said to her, "Daughter, your faith has made you well; go in peace, and be healed of your disease."

—Mark 5:34

How many of us live in "dis-ease," a state of feeling uneasy, uncomfortable, distressed, or just "not right"? Sometimes we don't know why we feel this way, but at other times it may be because we're living with an ongoing low level of stress that we don't know how to release. Are we open to believing that this dis-ease we live with doesn't have to be? If we do as the woman in the Scripture with the hemorrhage and tell God the "whole story," believing that we can be healed, perhaps we can surrender ourselves to healing. Ask and believe!

"Dear God, our great physician, I know that you can heal me, but I struggle with whether I really want to be healed. It's so easy to get used to stress and living in ways that aren't helpful to me. And yet it's so hard to change! I do want to be healed—help me to want it all the time, even if it requires me to make changes in my life. Help me to be whole and at peace, healed of all the ways I work against myself."

I Will Give You Rest

"My presence will go with you, and I will give you rest."

—Exodus 33:14

One of the most difficult experiences of being stressed is the feeling of being alone and even isolated in our struggle. For most of us, there's no substitute for the support we receive when someone who cares about us is close by. While we know in our minds that we are always in God's presence, we also need to experience it. We can intensify our awareness of resting in the real presence of God by closing our eyes and quieting ourselves. With each breath, we can imagine that God is holding us close and giving us rest from all that is distressing us. As we exhale, we might imagine letting go of all of our tension and watching it dissipate in the air around us.

"O God in whom I live and move and have my being, I know that you are with me. I am especially aware now of resting in your presence as I release through my breath all the tension and tightness I have been carrying. With each breath I take in, help me to know that I'm filling myself up with your love and blessing. Every once in a while throughout this day, help me call to mind the image of myself resting in your presence. I see myself being held by you as each breath brings me the serenity of your presence."

PEACE I LEAVE WITH YOU

*"Peace I leave with you; my peace I give to you.
I do not give to you as the world gives. Do not let your hearts
be troubled, and do not let them be afraid."*

—JOHN 14:27

Too often in our lives, we see ourselves as victims. We feel traumatized by life and look for the causes of our distress outside ourselves. How interesting that Jesus reminds us that his gift to us is a gift of peace. With a real belief in that gift to support us, we can then listen to the words that follow, when he points out what our responsibility is in finding peace—not allowing our hearts to be troubled or to be afraid. So we may be able to surrender our stress when we make a real decision to *not* allow trouble and fear into our experience.

"God of peace, remind me that you've given me the gift of peace at every moment. I can choose to ignore your gift and wallow in my fear and distress, or I can open my mind and heart to receive it—it's up to me. When I'm feeling stressed and upset, I will pray, 'God of peace, I rest in you,' and repeat it until it becomes my experience."

The Lord Will Guide You

The LORD will guide you continually,
and satisfy your needs in parched places.

—Isaiah 58:11

So often life feels like a "parched" or desert place for us—dry, without consolation or comfort, and even dangerous at times. We may feel trapped, without direction, and helpless to change things. Sometimes our situations scare us, and we don't know where to find help. We might remind ourselves that real desert places are full of life, full of creatures that have learned to thrive in the dryness. God lives in desert places as well as in darkness. It's often in those dark and parched times, when we recognize our need and ask for help, that we find the healing that God is offering us.

"Jesus, I give you my hand as I stumble through the hard places of my life. Please don't let go of me, even if I seem at times to pull away from you. Help me know that you are close and that you always offer me the gifts of growth and healing that I need in these hard times. I may need to seek help from others to find my way and to learn from the stresses in my life. Please work through these people to guide me."

Give Thanks to the Lord

I will give thanks to the Lord with my whole heart.
—Psalm 111:1

Each event and experience that life offers us is an opportunity for growth in holiness. However, we do have the choice of refusing the new life that presents itself to us. God never forces anything on us. It takes some effort to begin to see difficulties as potential blessings. We must be willing to change our ways of thinking and judging. Of course, it's easier to be grateful for things we enjoy, but our challenge is to be able to find the gift in those things that are difficult.

"I want to be able to thank you for everything, Lord, even those hard things in my life. Help me see the value of those gifts that I would rather give back to you— how they challenge me and force me to depend on you and my brothers and sisters in Christ. I know that you are hidden in these challenges, so help me to be even more grateful for them than I am for all those gifts I so eagerly accept from you. I do thank you with my whole heart."

CHOOSE LOVE

Above all, clothe yourselves with love,
which binds everything together in perfect harmony.

—COLOSSIANS 3:14

Love is a choice. Too often we wait for love to come, and usually expect to know it by the feelings it evokes rather than by the choices and decisions we make. We may never have thought of love as an antidote for stress. And yet, here is St. Paul, telling us that if we choose to love, even when stress is pulling us apart, we are on our way to perfect harmony. Who wouldn't want to make a choice like that?

"God, whose name is love, help me to choose well. But first, help me to know that I can make a choice for love in my life. I can be a loving person each day—choosing always for the highest good for myself and others. May I think of you each morning as I awake, and ask for your help in choosing to clothe myself in love. May that love then mean blessing for others, and harmony and blessing for me."

Wait in Silence for God

For God alone my soul waits in silence;
from him comes my salvation.

—Psalm 62:1

One of the most powerful methods of coping when stress is running high is to sit quietly in God's presence. As we empty our minds, we can stop the frenetic worries and thoughts that battle for attention. It's been said that silence is God's primary language. When we are willing to encounter God in such a manner, we find ourselves calmed by the silence we share. Then we know that we are now with God, speaking the same language.

I sit comfortably, preferably upright, and close my eyes to minimize distractions. I take a deep breath to fill my lungs and heart, exhale, and then let my breathing become even and regular. I recall that God is already here, simply waiting for me to be consciously aware of that truth. Instead of telling God how to manage my problems, I simply say, "God, you love me more than I can imagine. Teach me and show me the way." I may repeat this prayer several times as I sit and breathe quietly, or I may simply sit in silence, aware that I am in the loving presence of God.

TURN FEAR INTO TRUST

In God, whose word I praise,
in God I trust; I am not afraid.

—PSALM 56:4

Pervasive and all-consuming fear can wreak havoc in our lives. When it is our constant companion, then everything worries us and begins to take on the guise of a threat. Fear can paralyze us as we attempt to avoid everything distressing. When we find ourselves avoiding even those challenges that are important to our growth, then fear has become a major obstacle for us on our personal journey. Instead of giving way to fear, perhaps we will take reasonable cautions as wisdom teaches us, and then affirm the profound truth that "in God I trust; I am not afraid."

"My Lord and my God, when I feel afraid, guide me to turn that fear into trust in you. Teach me to notice when fear begins to arise in me, and then remind me that I can use it as an opportunity to draw closer to you. Show me if there is anything I need to do to deal with those things that frighten me, and then help me hand the situation over to you, my God. I will affirm over and over the words of the psalmist: 'In God I trust; I am not afraid.'"

God's Peace Surpasses Understanding

And the peace of God, which surpasses all understanding,
will guard your hearts and your minds in Christ Jesus.

—Philippians 4:7

We live in a world that becomes more frenetic day by day, in which we find ourselves running around trying to do more and more. So we pride ourselves on our ability to multitask. What about priding ourselves instead on our ability to create a peaceful environment in our beings? What about giving our hearts and minds an occasional break from the frenzy? How often do we hear ourselves saying something like "If only I could have a little peace"? What about making that a priority? What about choosing to take a few minutes when we "rest" in the peace of God within us?

"Here I am, my God of peace, simply closing my eyes and resting in you. Here I am, aware of your renewing me with every breath I take and release. May I be as good at resting in your peace with you as I am at being efficient and productive with my day. I will try to turn to you periodically throughout the day as I take a deep breath, close my eyes, and ask that my heart and mind be renewed in you."

THE SPIRIT HELPS US IN OUR WEAKNESS

Likewise the Spirit helps us in our weakness;
for we do not know how to pray as we ought, but that very Spirit
intercedes with sighs too deep for words. And God, who searches the
heart, knows what is the mind of the Spirit.

—ROMANS 8:26-27

Imagine how much relief we would find from our stresses and worries if we took these words from St. Paul to heart. The fact is that even when I don't know what I need, the Spirit of God does know, and is asking for just such a gift for me. And God, who hears the Spirit, is providing what the Spirit is asking for me. What a blessing to us! We only have to agree to what the Spirit is asking. Can we say yes to whatever that gift might be?

"God of love, so many times I place the whole responsibility for my life on my own shoulders. At such moments I feel such a heavy burden and wish that I knew what was best for me. I crave some direction—someone to tell me what to do and how to proceed—and then for help to do it. I tend to forget that you and the Holy Spirit are right now within and all around me, moving me in the way I should go. I choose right now to say yes to you and your plan for my life. And my God, I count on your help as I 'live and move and have my being' in you" (see Acts 17:28).

Deliverance Is Nearer Than We Think

*Always remember that this is the hour of crisis, it is high time
for you to wake out of sleep, for deliverance is nearer to us now
than it was when first we believed.*

—Romans 13:11, REB

When have you found yourself in an "hour of crisis"? In such times, we often experience a loss of some kind or the death of someone or something we love. But in the empty space of that loss, we can ask Jesus to bring us new life. We can be born again through such experiences. These hours of crisis can be such important times in our faith journey if we are alert and awake to the possibilities. Even though the crisis may be a painful one, we can choose to be born again through this difficulty and come to new life through Christ who lives in us.

"Every moment in my sacred journey, I want to choose to grow closer to you, dear Jesus. I realize that my crises and troubles are the very stuff out of which you can bring that growth. As life presents me with any kind of suffering, and as I invite suffering on occasion through my own poor decisions, may I be open to all the ways you will draw me closer to you and help me to grow. So here I am, with my eyes wide open. Be with me through all my hours of crisis."

Let Go of Distress

O Lord, what are human beings that you regard them,
or mortals that you think of them?
They are like a breath;
their days are like a passing shadow.

—Psalm 144:3-4

Sometimes we make so much of things. Someone affronts us, and we blow the situation way out of proportion to what actually occurred. We may spend days feeling upset and offended. Friends and family members stop speaking to each other, each one waiting for the other to apologize. Love and forgiveness are hovering around the fringes, and we leave them unacknowledged. How sad for everyone involved, whose days are "a passing shadow." May we not waste our days by clinging to distress.

"My life is so short, my God. Please help me to not let it waste away in hard feelings. I am the one who needs to choose to be a loving person. No one else can make me be loving, or make me act in an unloving way, no matter what that person says or does. When I've been wronged or feel distressed, let me take a breath and make a decision to respond in love."

RESCUE ME, GOD, FROM MY TROUBLES

The salvation of the righteous is from the LORD;
he is their refuge in the time of trouble.

—PSALM 37:39

Where do we tend to turn when we know we're in trouble? And do we find help? Sometimes we turn to things that can only intensify or complicate the problem. If we use drugs or alcohol to blunt our awareness, as we come out on the other side, we find we have created a greater problem. Ignoring the trouble may only make it worse. Pretending it isn't there prolongs the journey to healing. It could be helpful for us to think about our usual ways of reacting. Do they help?

"Come to my rescue, God, my help, whenever I'm in trouble. Turn me away from my tendency to block or avoid my difficulties. With you at my side, I can gain perspective on my problems and look for healthy ways to resolve them. I may even be able to grow through them. May I always turn to you first."

Fear No Evil

Even though I walk through the darkest valley,
    I fear no evil;
for you are with me;
    your rod and your staff—
        they comfort me.   —Psalm 23:4

All of us find ourselves in dark valleys at various times in our lives. Sometimes these valleys have the power to trip us up or undermine our efforts to do good. When we can't seem to find our way through them, they scare us. That's when we need something to hold on to, something to support and comfort us and lead us to safe ground. These are the times to reach for God's hand, to grab hold of the staff held out to us to keep us steady. Sometimes God's hand comes in the form of human help, and in those times we are grateful those who walk with us through the darkness, so that we are not alone.

"Even in my darkest valleys, when I feel so alone and fear that I'll never make my way out, God of my life, you are there. Give me first a willingness to think about you, to remind myself for even the hundredth time that there is no place where you are not. Then give me brothers and sisters to walk with me in my darkness. Lord, I purposefully surrender my fears and despair to you. In my mind, I choose to give you my hand, to hold fast to you, knowing that you will never leave me in darkness. You will never abandon me. I count on you."

Pray for One Another

"Therefore . . . pray for one another, so that you may be healed. The prayer of the righteous is powerful and effective."

—James 5:16

We all play a role in each other's lives, for good or for ill. As we each travel along our own sacred journey, who we are and what we do touch and affect the people around us, even when we aren't thinking consciously about it. What power for good we unleash when we choose to pray for each other, even just in passing. The prayerful concern of others for us and us for them would have a powerful effect on each of our lives.

"Holy Spirit, who knows my heart and mind, remind me frequently of the power for good that I can be through my prayers. Help me be more aware of that power. Lord, as I look around at so many people, some known to me and some unknown, I ask you to bless each one of them. I pray that they would, in their own unique way, manifest you in the world. I thank you for working through me to bring blessing to my brothers and sisters. May I be a positive force for good in their lives."

This Is the Day the Lord Has Made

This is the day that the Lord has made;
let us rejoice and be glad in it.

—Psalm 118:24

Every day is a day that the Lord has made. And whatever each day holds is the raw material from which we make our lives and re-create ourselves. So each day is precious. Each day offers us experiences and events that may be enjoyable or challenging. No matter how we describe what is going on in our lives—likeable or distressing—all our experiences offer us an opportunity. Eventually we come to see that it isn't what happens in our lives that helps or hurts us, but rather what we do with it.

"Help me, my ever-present God, to come to see that every day is a one-of-a-kind opportunity to celebrate the blessings you offer me. Some blessings come in delightful packages while others come wrapped in hard times. Both kinds can lead to growth. Give me eyes to see that truly each day is a day made by you, and that you will always walk with me as I travel it. Help me, then, to live each day well, and to be able to rejoice and be glad in each one that's given to me."

WITH YOUR BURDEN GO TO GOD

"Come to me, all you that are weary and are carrying heavy burdens, and I will give you rest."

—MATTHEW 11:28

Who among us has not at some time in our lives felt the pressure and strain of heavy burdens? Even little children suffer from worries and distress. Life is often marked by pain and sorrow, by struggle and need, by difficulties and ailments. No one seems exempt. Even though life can also hold a great deal of delight and enjoyment, we become weary by the burdens we each try to carry. We need to know that God notices—notices our burdens and notices our weariness—and calls us to come close to him and find rest.

"Dear God, I know what it feels like when someone offers me help with a heavy load and takes some of the burden from me. I immediately notice how much lighter the load becomes. Through these words of Jesus, that's what you are offering me. So I come to you, Lord, and I thank you for carrying my burdens of worry and distress. Let me think of you standing close to me, holding me up, as well as my heavy burden. I know that without you, I would never make it through even one day."

LIVE IN PEACE

Live in peace; and the God of love and peace will be with you.
—2 CORINTHIANS 13:11

Peace is an "inside job," which means that peace is often the result of our attempts to live that way. We can cultivate peace in many ways. One way is by working to live peacefully with everyone we encounter each day. To do so, we need to be willing and eager to ask for forgiveness when we offend others and to accept forgiveness when it's offered to us. We can also consciously learn to become peaceful inwardly. This requires us to take the time to sit and bring to our minds images and thoughts that are calming to us. As we rest in these images, we can breathe in God's peace.

I sit in silence and quiet myself. Then I bring a peaceful image to my mind—perhaps a majestic mountain scene, a garden of roses, or the smiling face of a loved one. I also think peaceful thoughts: "I am peaceful and calm." "The God of peace holds me close." I inhale peace with every breath. As I rest in these images and thoughts, I pray, "Dear Lord, hold me close to your heart. I release any hurts or bitterness that I may be holding against someone. I want to live in peace with you and with others, so I will ask forgiveness of anyone I have hurt. Throughout the day, may my affirmation be 'God of peace and love, I rest always in you.'"

Change Is Possible

"For God all things are possible."

—Mark 10:27

Sometimes it's easy to fool ourselves into believing that nothing can change and that things are as they always will be. But for change to happen, we have to want it to happen. Change often requires us to do things that are initially uncomfortable or difficult. We would rather believe that it's not possible for things to change, and so we stay set in our ways. If we want to release our attachments to stressful living, we have to do our part—God won't do it alone. We have to say yes to the change. So the question is this: Is the release of stress possible for us? Are we willing to say yes to such change? Are we willing to develop a more positive attitude toward the realities of life?

"I know that change is painful, and yet, dear God, I know that life is full of change. Since my birth, I've changed enormously, and I've watched everything change all around me. Loss is forever present, along with my futile efforts—and the stress that these efforts induce—to keep things as they are. I don't want to spend my life being chronically stressed. Help me to change both my attitude and the stubborn ways in which I create and maintain stress in my life. I want to be continually aware of your abundant gifts, O Lord, and have a grateful and peaceful heart that remains calm in you."

Go to the Mountain of God

*And after he had dismissed the crowds, he went up
the mountain by himself to pray.*

—Matthew 14:23

Mountains have often been places of pilgrimage where people
go in search of God. Perhaps that's because atop a mountain, we
feel closer to the heavens. After times of preaching and healing
and being with people in need, Jesus backed off from the crowds
and headed to the mountains to pray and restore himself. When
stress is a significant part of our lives, we each need a "mountain" where we can be nourished and restored; we need a place
to which we can withdraw. Perhaps we could schedule such times
and then keep those appointments, just as we would any other
important appointment we have. We may just find that Jesus has
already climbed that mountain and is waiting with open arms
to greet us.

"Jesus, teach me that it is just as important for me to
periodically withdraw from my life or my work as it
was for you. I need to take time to move away from all
the activities and stresses that are part of my everyday
responsibilities in this world. Not only will I be able to
handle them better when I've had some respite, but I
will also find myself rejuvenated and nourished from
my closeness with you."

The Lord Is Near

The LORD is near to the brokenhearted,
and saves the crushed in spirit.

—PSALM 34:18

How interesting that Jesus chose to spend more time with those in distress—the poor, the suffering, those who recognized they needed help—than with those who seemed less needy. The blind man who called out, the hemorrhaging woman who touched his clothing—all knew that they had needs. And they also knew that Jesus would help them. Do we recognize our need? Are we willing to ask for help? Or do we feel obliged to appear self-sufficient? When we are willing to see ourselves as needy, then we can ask for help.

"Jesus, even though I have been given many gifts, in many ways I am in need. Help me to recognize my needs, and help me to know that you are the one who has everything I need. Great God of abundance, I need you to think of me, or I will cease to exist. I need your presence, in which I live and move and have my being. I need your care for me, your love, your touch on everything I do. And when my spirit is crushed, you are the only one who can make me whole again."

God, Come Quickly to My Aid

O my God, I cry by day, but you do not answer;
and by night, but find no rest.
But you, O LORD, do not be far away!
O my help, come quickly to my aid!

—PSALM 22:2, 19

We may be so overwhelmed by our situations that we feel as if we're drowning in distress and have nothing to cling to. Sometimes even a sense of panic may settle in, and we feel desperate. The challenge for us in such times is to be able to recognize that no matter how distressed we are, God is right in the middle of it with us, present within the very turmoil. At the same time, we might develop some simple techniques, such as learning to replace our worrisome thoughts with those that are more soothing or calming.

"God, I tend to think that if you are present, everything will be pleasant and moving along well, and all will be at peace. Help me to remember that you are with me at every single moment, in the midst of every event and in every feeling I have. Even if I try, I cannot avoid you. Help me to remind myself of this reality when times are hard for me. Help me to stop and purposefully say, 'God, you are here . . . in this very place . . . at this very moment. You are loving me and holding me in your heart and hands. Help me.'"

God's Spirit upon Us

*The spirit of the Lord G*OD* is upon me.*

—ISAIAH 61:1

What does it mean to have the Spirit of the Lord upon us? If we really had eyes to see, we would be blinded by the radiance of God's love permeating our whole being. We would be caught up in that radiance pouring from us, dazzled by the love showered on us. No matter how many mistakes or poor decisions we've made, the loving presence of God surrounds us and holds us. How peaceful we would be if we kept this reality in mind! Not only would we be filled with God's love, but we would radiate that love to everyone we encounter.

"Wake me up, my radiant and loving God, and help me see that your Spirit is always upon me. Show me that when I welcome and acknowledge your presence with and in me, I will be carrying you to all those around me. May I be a conduit for you and for the work of your Spirit in this world. Help me to imagine myself as bringing you to those with whom I come into contact. Even in dealing with difficult situations, help me go inward and imagine your radiance as you flow out to others through me."

BECOME A PEACEMAKER

*A harvest of righteousness is sown in peace for
those who make peace.*

—JAMES 3:18

If we surveyed our own friends and family members, how many
of them would describe us as persons who influence others in
positive, life-giving ways? How many would give us high ratings
as those who build up others, who strive to be makers and sup-
porters of peace? How would we rank ourselves? Do we want
to be known as persons of peace, who actively contribute to the
creation of a peaceful, life-giving atmosphere around us?

"God of peace, I want to be called your child. I want to
consciously be one who values peace and works to create an atmosphere of peace wherever I am. I know that
if I want to be a peacemaker, I must begin that work
in my own heart so that I am peaceful on the inside as
well as the outside. Help me to be your child, a peacemaker who reflects your peace as you shine through
me wherever I go."

The Gift of Challenges

My child, when you come to serve the Lord,
prepare yourself for testing.

—Sirach 2:1

Life challenges everyone, and how we struggle and cope with these challenges contributes to how we grow. When we're willing to look at our struggles and stresses as testing times rather than as punishments or afflictions, we begin to see their significance and the opportunities they offer. Our chance to grow begins with our willingness to redefine the stressful situations. When we see them differently, we cope with them differently.

"Open the eyes of my mind, dear God, so that I am able to see that everything life presents to me is not only an opportunity for me to be tested but also to grow closer to you. Help me to not become discouraged, but to view this testing as a way for you to make me stronger and a more committed follower of your Son, Jesus."

An Everlasting Love

I have loved you with an everlasting love;
therefore I have continued my faithfulness to you.
—Jeremiah 31:3

In a world in which half of all marriages fall apart, in which relationships are "on" one day and "off" the next, we crave the stability of loving someone who is always willing to love us in return. Much of our stress can arise when we feel unloved or unlovable. Perhaps we need to look at the choices offered to us every day to reach out in love. We might think of love as only a feeling and miss the reality that love becomes more apparent in our lives when we choose to be loving. When we grow in awareness of God's continued belief in us and love of us, we are so much more able to make the choice, not only to love ourselves, but also to reach out in love to others.

"My God, whose name is love, who is love, help me be aware each day of the choices before me. I can remind myself of your promise that your love is with me always. Grounded in that truth, I can then make open and conscious choices to be loving in a particular situation or with a particular person in my life. In choosing to behave that way, I can be the place you use to be present to the people I encounter."

Give Thanks to the Lord

It is good to give thanks to the Lord,
to sing praises to your name, O Most High.

—Psalm 92:1

When we get so caught up in complaining and distress, we miss opportunities to give thanks to God. We are laden with gifts of all kinds, both around us and within us. If we cultivate the ability to be grateful and to say thanks, we can live our lives with joy and delight in what we have, rather than with resentment about what we don't have. We might even begin to see that it's better in many instances not to have—and to be grateful for the richness of that reality.

"Forgive me, my generous God, for failing to notice and thank you for all the gifts in my life. Help me to guard my mind and tongue when I am tempted to complain or become negative. Put joy in my heart each day so that I can delight in the beauty of my life and sing your praises for all that you do for me. Take away any resentment or anger about those situations I find difficult. Your plan for my life is perfect, and I trust in you, even when I don't understand it."

Turn Mourning into Joy

I will turn their mourning into joy,
I will comfort them, and give them gladness for
sorrow.

—Jeremiah 31:13

Mourning is a natural, integral part of life. Throughout our lives we will experience countless deaths and losses. We navigate our way through these losses by being able and willing to mourn them. However, mourning can be very stressful. Because it's painful and sad, or because we've never learned how necessary and healing mourning can be, we may try to avoid it. Or on the other hand, we may hold onto our mourning for fear of "forgetting" the memory of the person or the experience we have lost. If we give ourselves to our sadness and grieving, we can move forward to the new life that Christ has for us.

"How blessed I've been, O God, by all the gifts you've given me in my life. And how hard it is when it's time to let them go. I want joy and happiness again in my life, but my sadness and grief continue to cling to me. Help me to give myself fully over to my mourning for as long as I need to, and then help me to let it go. I want to learn to live well, in gratitude for the gifts I've received from you and in gratitude for the life that is still mine in this world. May I again be filled with joy and delight."

Let Gentleness Flourish

Let your gentleness be known to everyone.
—Philippians 4:5

Life can be rough and difficult. We tend to operate in a competitive, power-based way in order to get ahead and "win." Most of us live in pressure-filled environments, trying to do far more than we have the time or energy to manage. Multitasking has us going in all directions at once. We're often at war with ourselves, stealing time from one area that we can't afford to give up, and using it in another area that needs more than we can contribute. We allow little time for rest or recuperation, and we continue on with what we believe is expected of us. We show minimal gentleness with ourselves, not to mention others, but we keep pushing. Can we begin to welcome gentleness into our lives? Imagine the blessed relief experienced by others and ourselves if we do so.

"Holy Spirit, you who are the Spirit of gentleness, I invite and welcome you into my life. Somehow I know that gentleness is so much more healing, so much more comforting, and so much more helpful than the harshness I struggle with when I push myself and others. I know that when I'm around gentle people, their gentleness rubs off on to me. I also know that my gentleness nurtures more peace in others than when I'm sharp or bossy. Help me to cultivate gentleness. Make it part of my interactions with all the people in my life, and also with myself. May I be blessed with your spirit of gentleness."

THE LORD IS WITH YOU

I will never forget you.

—Isaiah 49:15, NAB

Most of us know what it's like to feel forgotten. Friends, family members, or co-workers, caught up in the busyness of their own lives, scurry right past us and our aching needs or worries. Sometimes all we crave is for someone to simply be willing to be present and attentive to us. What would we feel in these times if we really believed that God is more tuned into our worry than we are?

"Lord, you know me better than I know myself. You are more aware of my life and concerns than I am and know them inside out in ways I tend to avoid. Remind me that you are aware of me at every moment. It is you and your care for me that keep me in existence at every single moment. My very life and being are sustained by you and your promise to never forget me. I, too, want to never forget you."

God's Covenant of Peace

My steadfast love shall not depart from you,
and my covenant of peace shall not be removed.

—Isaiah 54:10

Covenants need assent and agreement from both sides. If we accept the reality of a covenant of peace between God and us, then we must do our part to support and build up that covenant. God's intention and commitment are rock solid. So what about our side of this covenant—do we want and choose to be at peace? Would we rather be grumbling and unhappy about life, complaining about how hard things are? Or might we say, "God of peace, help us to not depart from you. Make us strong in our commitment and connection to you in our covenant of peace."

In my imagination, I envision myself sitting in the midst of God's bright light of peace. I involve all of my senses: I see the brightness, feel the softness of God's touch, hear the quiet music of his voice, smell the scent of flowers everywhere. Then I say, "God of peace and love, may your steadfast love permeate my experience. May I release all the thoughts and concerns that try to keep me from this peaceful place."

In Your Trouble, Call to God

Call on me in the day of trouble;
I will deliver you, and you shall glorify me.

—Psalm 50:15

Have you ever said to yourself, "I'm really in trouble. I have no idea how I'm going to handle this problem"? Trouble can come into our lives in so many ways—sometimes totally unexpectedly—and when it does, we can feel overwhelmed and helpless. These are the times when we must acknowledge our helplessness and call out to God. Every one of these circumstances can open us to new life and healing, but first we have to know that we're in need, and then we have to call out to God for deliverance. Finally, we need to trust in God delivering us and give him all the glory. This final step is an essential one.

"You've promised, God, that if I call upon you in my times of trouble, you will deliver me. Well, here I am, in great need of your help. I trust you will be with me, and I give you thanks with all my heart. I join my voice with the voices of all the saints in heaven and on earth to give you glory."

LIVE OUT GOD'S PLAN

For surely I know the plans I have for you, says the LORD,
plans for your welfare and not for harm, to give you a future
with hope. Then when you call upon me and come
and pray to me, I will hear you.

—JEREMIAH 29:11-12

As we move through our lives, we hope that we are becoming the person that God had in mind when he created us. Our experiences are varied—some pleasant and enjoyable and full of delight, some full of pain and sorrow. How we become the person God intended us to be is tied into how we cope with what life offers us—the enjoyable as well as the difficult. At the most basic level, we must recognize that this is simply the way life is. And even in our most painful times, our challenge is to maintain hope, choose not to give way to despair, and call on God, who promises to be with us and hear our prayer.

"Heavenly Father, sometimes I struggle with why things are so hard in my life. I keep thinking that I must have done something wrong and that you must be punishing me. But I need to realize that life has its ups and downs, and that the "down" times are not always the result of some failure of mine. Show me how to live well, even when life is challenging. You have promised to hear me, and I know that promise is true."

You Are Wonderfully Made

I praise you, for I am fearfully and wonderfully made.

—Psalm 139:14

What amazing creatures we are! We don't have to tell our hearts to beat, our lungs to breathe, or our stomachs to digest our food. Emotionally we cope with losses and disappointments, sickness and aging, injuries and sadness, and we move forward with our lives, even when things are tough. God has made us resilient, resourceful, and creative in finding ways to live and cope with difficulties. We can have confidence in his design of us.

"I thank you, God, for all the ways you have designed me. Thank you so much for how your creation flourishes, even without our conscious knowledge. Thank you for giving me ways to cope with my hardships, whether that be in the way others support me or through your presence in my life. I remain in awe of all the ways I am so wonderfully made."

Live in Love

Children, love must not be a matter of theory or talk; it must be true love which shows itself in action.

—1 John 3:18, REB

Stress is often the result of relationship difficulties. Perhaps we've argued with another person, or become angry about some misunderstanding or difference of opinion. As our feelings go awry, we don't feel very loving. Maybe we think that our love is dependent on the feelings we have for another person. This may be the time to realize that our love is shown by the way we choose to face or deal with the other person, even when we don't feel very loving. If we choose to act with love, we can also relieve the stresses we feel in that situation.

"Dear God, whose name is love, help me to always respond with love, even when I don't feel very loving. Let me recognize that love is at work when I am concerned about the well-being of the other person and act in his or her best interest. May all my interactions with others be based on real love for them and for myself, even when I'm feeling angry or uncomfortable. If I act in love, then I'll have nothing to regret."

Turn to God

Turn to me and be gracious to me,
for I am lonely and afflicted.
Relieve the troubles of my heart,
and bring me out of my distress.

—Psalm 25:16-17

The "troubles of my heart" may take on different forms, but at any given time in our lives, we can name at least one worry or problem we count as "trouble." In fact, life can be overwhelming with the situations and circumstances that come to us. By recognizing the red flags that mark the approach of trouble, we can sometimes head off a problem and make a course correction. And one of the most helpful ways we can bring ourselves out of our sense of loneliness and helplessness is by turning to God. Asking straight out for what we need has an impact on our own mental state and also is a way to bring God into our situation.

"Here I am, my God, at your doorstep. It's hard to be in such distress and to feel so alone. When I call on you, I know in my heart that immediately I'm not alone anymore. I'm aware that there is no way you can or will not hear me. When I talk over my troubles with you, I begin to see them from a new perspective. Other possibilities may arise in my heart or mind that open new avenues for me. In any case, it's my troubles and distress that have brought me to your presence. They may provide my first step in coming into peace again."

Pursue a Foundation of Peace

Pursue peace with everyone.

—Hebrews 12:14

When we were growing up, most of us were told to be polite and respectful—and most of us try to do that. But what if we were also told to pursue peace with everyone? How would we do that? What are the attitudes and habits that we would begin to incorporate into our basic interactions with others? Maybe compassion and loving kindness would underlie and set the stage for all the rest of our actions and responses. What a beautiful foundation we would have as we interacted with each person we encountered!

"Help me make the pursuit of peace a basic goal in all of my interactions, God. Let me be conscious of it as I move into any discussion or interchange with anyone. And help me to make it a significant and always present component of all my conversations and discussions. Let it become second nature to me, so that none of my energy is wasted on battling with other people. Even when we disagree, let the pursuit of peace be at the very center of our encounters."

God's Angels Guard You

For he will command his angels concerning you
to guard you in all your ways.
On their hands they will bear you up.

—Psalm 91:11-12

No matter what we may be experiencing, no matter how lost we feel or anxious or worried or overwhelmed, we can count on the fact that an angel is with us. We're immersed in the presence of God and in the company of powerful spiritual beings who have been "commanded" to guard us, not only when we're in distress, but in "all our ways." What a gift to us! And how often do we even acknowledge the presence of the angels?

"Angel of God, my companion and guardian at every moment, I greet you and thank you for your constant care of me. Please forgive my inattention to you. As I sit here quietly now, I know that you are delighted that I'm aware of you and am speaking to you. Like the psalmist, I count on you to guard me and bear me up. Protect me from evil. May I always remember to call on you when I need protection and care."

Tell God What You Need

Do not worry about anything, but in everything
by prayer and supplication with thanksgiving let your
requests be made known to God.

—Philippians 4:6

Seriously examining a problem—or seeking help in resolving difficulties—is not the same as worrying, which tends only to keep us agitated and upset. Worrying is often directed toward all the "what ifs" of our lives, and the "if onlys" that accompany them, and often focuses on things over which we have no control. How can we break this habit, which only creates more stress for us and wastes so much energy? St. Paul urges us to tell God what we need. As we do so, we should give thanks, showing that we are in fact already confident that God will answer our prayers. What an effective antidote to worry!

"Lord, you know me. You know that I am always tempted to worry. Help me to see how unproductive it is to worry about things over which I have no control. When I find myself worrying, I turn to you and make my requests known to you. As I would talk with a friend who is at my side, I will talk with you. Then I will praise and thank you in advance for hearing my prayers. I know that you will answer me. Lord, I trust in you."

Live with Joy

For you shall go out in joy,
  and be led back in peace;
the mountains and the hills before you
  shall burst into song.

—Isaiah 55:12

When our attention is focused on things that are painful, difficult, or sad, we often miss opportunities that are all around us to experience joy. Yet joy has been called the infallible sign of God's presence. Joy doesn't have to be overly exuberant and demonstrative. We can live with a quiet joy just under the surface of our daily lives. The softness of the breeze caressing our faces, the songs of the birds, or the sight of a sleeping infant can bring delight to our hearts. We might begin by becoming more aware of the things that give us joy. Then we can welcome the joy that we feel, opening our arms to it and giving it a home in our hearts.

"Open my eyes, my God of beautiful creation, and don't let me miss the joy that is around me. Teach me to be like you and to delight in what you've made. I choose to not spend too much time dwelling on sadness and distress. Fill me with joy so that I may find many reasons to burst into song with you in my heart."

Relieve My Troubles, O Lord

*When the righteous cry for help, the L*ORD *hears,*
and rescues them from all their troubles.

—Psalm 34:17

Everyone has troubles. Sometimes we invite troubles by the choices we make, and sometimes they just come of their own accord. It seems no life is without them, and they can make us feel as if we are sinking into a quagmire. Perhaps we can deal with troubles in several different ways. We can deal with them directly by acknowledging them, asking for help, and working at loosening their grip on our lives. We can also change our perspective on them. Instead of seeing our troubles in a negative way, we might look at them with new eyes and recognize the opportunities they bring for challenging our growth and bringing us closer to the Lord.

"God, please take away my troubles, but not before I find the strength to manage them and grow through them. Sharpen my way of looking at my struggles so that I see the gift hidden in them—the gift that will bring me new growth and a closer relationship with you."

Desire What God Wants

And going a little farther, he threw himself on the ground and prayed, "My Father, if it is possible, let this cup pass from me; yet not what I want but what you want."

—Matthew 26:39

Life can unexpectedly ask of us something we believe is so big and so overwhelming that we don't think we can handle it. We cry out to be relieved of the pain, to be removed from the situation, or to be exonerated. We know that we can't manage it ourselves and feel deeply our helplessness and vulnerability. That's the moment when we recognize that the only way we are going to survive the situation is to throw ourselves on the mercy of God. How close we can be at such times to the pain of Jesus' own struggle in the Garden of Gethsemane as we finally acknowledge, as he did, that the only real surrender possible is to what God wants.

"God of mercy, you know my pain! I am bereft of any comfort or peace, and feel totally unable to change things myself. Save me from the depths of my distress. Please remove from me the cause of my great suffering, and let me find rest in you. You can save me if you will. But let me add, from my broken heart, that I trust you will carry me through this pain. So I ask to let be whatever is your will. You will give me strength."

CREATE PEACE ON EARTH

"Blessed are the peacemakers,
for they will be called children of God."

—MATTHEW 5:9

We tend to not give much thought to the impact we have on the people and the world around us. We see ourselves as individuals, living our own lives as others live theirs. Yet we profoundly affect and influence each other just by being who we are. We pass through the lives of negative and angry people, feeling the effect of their attitudes on us even when we don't consciously think about it. In the same fashion, we are affected by the attitudes of those in a more positive and contented state. We each help create not only our own world but the worlds of others who pass through or share our lives.

"Creator God, help me realize that I, too, help create the lives of other people by who I am. The people I spend time with are contributing to who I am as well. Wake me up to the ways we influence each other. I want to live in ways that help others grow and become all that they can be, and I want to be aware of how others are influencing me. You clearly encourage us to create peace on this earth. You even call peacemakers 'children of God.' Help me to be a member of that group. "

The Spirit Lives within You

I will put my spirit within you, and you shall live.

—Ezekiel 37:14

We don't seem to realize that without the spirit of God in us on a daily basis, we could never exist! At every given moment—whether we're having fun or are in pain, whether we're serious or silly, whether we're wide awake or fast asleep—we are being kept alive by the spirit of God that is in us. Why don't we think about this amazing reality when we're upset, distressed, sad, or even when we're filled with delight? How blessed we will be if we nurture an abiding awareness that it is God who sustains our lives, and that he is in us and with us at every moment, every day of our lives.

"Holy Spirit of God, you fill me with yourself, with your presence. Wake me up! Help me to acknowledge your presence far more than I do now. I want to talk with you as a friend. Each morning I want to thank you for being with me through the night. Even when I'm not thinking of you, you are here. So today, as I perform my duties, every once in a while let me think of you and how close you are to me. Open my ears and my heart, and let me be alert to what you might be saying to me. Thank you."

Receive God's Joy

I know that there is nothing better for them than to be happy and enjoy themselves as long as they live.

—Ecclesiastes 3:12

We may have grown up with the idea that life is always meant to be difficult. We may hear others say that God must want us to struggle and even suffer. How, then, do we explain these words from Ecclesiastes encouraging happiness and enjoyment? Do we believe that God wants us to have an abundant life, filled with his gifts for us? Are we open to finding the delight all around us and even in us? Maybe we need to give ourselves permission to enjoy ourselves as we take notice of and delight in the many gifts that God showers on us each day.

"May I recognize the importance of the expectations I create for myself each day. God, help me to develop a positive and life-giving attitude that will be the foundation on which I act and will show itself in everything I do. Holy Spirit, may I experience the fruit of the Spirit that is joy, and find the delight that is possible all around me."

Welcome God's Wisdom

*If any of you is lacking in wisdom, ask God, who gives to all
generously and ungrudgingly, and it will be given you.*

—James 1:5

Try as we might, most of us find ourselves less wise than we would
like to be. We make decisions on the spur of the moment. We get
overwhelmed by the flurry of activities and responsibilities that
press in on us. We struggle to find the answers for our dilemmas
as we slog through all the information before us. Popular problem solvers promise quick fixes based on the latest trends. Perhaps
the first thing we should do is slow down and remind ourselves
that wisdom is what is called for in our current situation. And
then we can ask God to give us the wisdom we need.

"God of wisdom, you who *are* Wisdom, surround me
and guide me. May I find you already within me, already
sharing yourself with me. Open me to the wisdom that
addresses my struggles and answers questions, even
before I ask. In this present difficulty of mine, as I am
more and more open to receiving your wisdom, may
I begin to see a resolution. Help me to recognize the
ways you speak to me and answer my call."

Seek the Help You Need

"Search, and you will find."

—Matthew 7:7

We often fail to see that we *do* have choices we can make when we feel highly stressed. We can focus on how terrible we feel, how huge our problems are, how overwhelmed we are, and how no one understands us or the problems we have. And we may be right! Life can be so hard sometimes, and usually there is no clear road map for how to resolve our difficulties. One choice we can make, however, is to seek help. All around us are people who would lend us a hand if we would just ask them. We can also adopt new ways of thinking and take concrete steps that lead us in new directions. And we can turn to Jesus, who hears our plea for help and once said, "Search, and you will find."

"Help me, Lord, not to get bogged down in my stresses. Help me know that besides trusting in you, I also have to do my part in making it through my distress. To begin with, I must show loving and healthy compassion for myself. Help me, then, to seek out and find sources of help in the good people all around me. Admitting that I need help might just be the first and best thing I can do for myself. Be there for me, God. Be in my searching. And then let me have eyes to see you, all around me, shining through in others."

WITHDRAW INTO PEACE

He would withdraw to deserted places and pray.

—LUKE 5:16

We often find ourselves overwhelmed with busyness and activity. Rarely are we alone, and rarely are our minds free from distractions. We overschedule ourselves with plans, activities, and a long to-do list. When we push one problem out of the way, another one rushes in. With such a constant internal clamor, we can't find peace. What if we find for ourselves a "deserted place" where we might spend even a little bit of time? When we place ourselves in a setting that is conducive to quietness and prayer—our backyard, an empty room, a walk in the woods or mountains—we give ourselves a huge gift. Even if we go there for only five minutes each day, we will be giving ourselves a chance at peace.

"God of silence and peace, here I am in this special place with only you. I sit comfortably, and breathe slowly and deeply. I come to you, not with a lot of words, but only with a deep desire to be with you. Sit with me. Allow my body and mind to relax in the knowledge that you are here with me. Help me know that I don't have to be stressed. Rather, you've encouraged me to be at peace in your presence."

Wrapped in God's Love

For I am convinced there is nothing in death or life, in the world
as it is or the world as it shall be, in the forces of the universe, in
heights or depths—nothing in all creation that can separate us
from the love of God in Christ Jesus our Lord.

—Romans 8:38-39, REB

If we are big-time worriers, we could profit from these words of
St. Paul. Being separated from the love of God is a true cause for
worry—if it were possible. But it's not. Here Paul tells us that
despite all the things we could think of to worry about, *nothing*
can take away from us this truth: that no matter what, we are
forever wrapped in the love of God.

"Lord, help me to discover that when I am covered by
your love, I have nothing to fear. If all the great forces of
the universe cannot separate me from your love, then nei-
ther can all those many smaller things that cause me to
worry. Help me to take the power out of all the threats
and problems I've allowed to undermine me. Your love
is always holding me in your great embrace."

REJOICE IN GOD'S FAVOR

"Greetings, favored one! The Lord is with you."

—LUKE 1:28

How important it is to be aware that an angel could speak to each of us these same words that announced the coming of Jesus to Mary. Through his incarnation, Jesus truly is with each one of us. We give God a place to be alive in this world—to see through our eyes and touch with our hands and reach out to others in love and care. We can say in response to this greeting, "Welcome, dear God of love! Thank you for being alive in me."

"Use my eyes, O God, to see the beauty of this world
    you have made.
Use my mouth to speak lovingly to those all around
    me.
Use my heart to express love to all of your creation.
Use my hands to touch your creation with respect
    and delight.
Use my mind to let go of my painful, clinging ways.
Use my whole being as a place where you can live and
    be loved.
And thank you for making each of us your 'favored
    one.'"

Let God Comfort You

As a mother comforts her child,
so will I comfort you.

—Isaiah 66:13

A child in distress surely touches a mother's heart. The mother, lovingly bonded to the child, hears the cry and reaches out to bring her little one close to her. Attuned to the discomfort that the child is suffering, the mother uses all the ways she knows to resolve the problem and remove the distress. What an image Scripture uses to describe God's own response when one of us is suffering—of God, bonded to us, hearing our distress and reaching out to hold us close, looking for ways to "make it better"! Knowing this is God's promised response, perhaps we can remind ourselves to reach out to God and ask for help when it hurts.

"Loving God, you are both a mother and father to me. I want to reach out to you in all of my distress. I count on your being close and hearing my cry. Help me know, even when I may not see an outward sign of your presence and care, that you are holding me in your love and wanting with all your heart to bring me comfort."

THE GIFT OF EACH DAY

So teach us to count our days
that we may gain a wise heart.

—PSALM 90:12

The awareness that our lives are finite can enrich each day that we live. The wisdom that comes with this awareness has been an inspiration down through the ages. "*Carpe diem*!" or "Seize the day!" arose with a sense of the preciousness of each day. All we ever have is the present moment. Are we willing, then, to make the most of this very time? Life has been called "a parade of holy instants." When we are in the midst of difficult times, it may be helpful to remind ourselves that we should focus our attention on now—today. As the Jesuit mystic Henri Boulad noted, "The present moment brings me on a plate a hot, burning, absolutely new, and original message which can enrich me infinitely" (*All Is Grace: God and the Mystery of Time*).

"My always attentive God, the only place I can ever find you is right now. Please don't let me forget this truth. I can make this moment something important to me. Help me bring my attention to the time I have right here before me. As I'm willing to live so vitally in the present, you will enable me to release the thoughts that weigh me down."

Receive the Very Best of Gifts

*Grace, mercy, and peace from God the Father
and Christ Jesus our Lord.*

—1 Timothy 1:2

One way we can begin our prayer each day is to first remind ourselves that at this very moment, and at every single moment of our lives, we are receiving the very best of gifts. Freely given out of love, without any deserving on our part, God is showering upon each of us the very life we live, each breath we take, and all the world full of blessings and grace—even when our lives may be problematic and difficult. And in the midst of all these gifts is the gift of peace, nestled in the deepest part of ourselves, accessible to us through all that makes up our lives.

"God, wake me up this day and every day to the fact that I am surrounded and permeated by your grace, your love, and your presence. As I breathe, let each breath remind me that it's you and your grace I am inhaling that gives me life. Should you ever forget me for one instant, I would cease to exist. So let me welcome you with each breath I take. Let me thank you for your presence and all the graces you bring me. And God, let this very awareness of your life in me also help me be aware of you as my source of peace. May that peace support me through all that life asks of me, especially today. Thank you."

GIVE THANKS IN EVERYTHING

*Give thanks in all circumstances; for this is the will
of God in Christ Jesus for you.*

—1 THESSALONIANS 5:18

Too often we focus on the hard times and the stresses that arise
when things don't go the way we hope. We can experience stress
when we overlook the gifts and only see the problems. One idea
for releasing such stress is to set aside a time each day for acknowledging the positive gifts in our lives. Write down your blessings.
Express thanks to God for the gifts that are yours. Remember
this wise advice: "If the only prayer you ever say is 'thank you,'
that is enough."

"Gracious God, the giver of all gifts, help me to awaken
to all the gifts in my life. Give me a grateful spirit, a
spirit of loving-kindness, so that I notice how blessed
I am. May I be filled with gratitude to you. May I also
be willing to thank those around me, who often are the
source of blessing to me, even when I fail to notice. May
I enjoy the many gifts of everyday life."

Do Not Let Your Hearts Be Troubled

"Do not let your hearts be troubled,
and do not let them be afraid."

—John 14:27

How common it is to believe that we have no control over what or how our "hearts" feel. "I wish I didn't feel so troubled," we say, "but I just can't help it." Perhaps we can learn to move in the direction in which Jesus is inviting us here. We can begin by accepting the fear or distress we experience and by determining to learn from it. When fear arises, we can ask the Lord to show us why we are feeling this way. We may gain an important insight about ourselves or others by asking this question. Often when we simply acknowledge the feelings, they begin to diminish, and that very change may launch us in the direction of peacefulness.

"Lord, help me to see that I don't have to allow negative emotions to rule my life. Fear and troublesome feelings may be the beginning of my movement toward you and your peace. Help me to acknowledge my emotions rather than burying or denying them. Let me go to you for wisdom and insight about why I am feeling this way. With you at my side, these emotions will not have the final say in my life."

ENCOURAGE ONE ANOTHER

Therefore encourage one another and build up each other,
as indeed you are doing.

—1 THESSALONIANS 5:11

If we live long enough, we come to see that other people can bring us the best life has to offer or the most distressing and painful experiences. We surely know that we can be huge gifts to each other, and that we can also be the source of great unhappiness. How important for us to realize the power we have with each other to build up or break down! Whatever our behavior, as it influences others positively or negatively, so will it also have an effect on us.

"Help me to be an encouraging person, dear God, one who gives life rather than diminishes it. Many of us are struggling every day to live as well as we can. We find ourselves with all kinds of worry and distress. Please bless those who have been full of encouragement for me, and help me notice all the small and large ways that I can be encouraging and supportive to others. What wonderful opportunities I will have, not only to bring a blessing to others, but also to receive blessings!"

God Hears Your Cries

Out of the depths I cry to you, O LORD.
Lord, hear my voice!

—PSALM 130:1-2

Rare is the person who hasn't experienced intermittent periods of darkness or being in "the depths." Crying out to God for help when we're in dark times acknowledges that we know we're not there alone. God doesn't avoid the darkness of our lives but instead hears our cries. Too many times we turn in other directions for help—to addictions or other unhealthy habits or pastimes—that can offer no healing. How important for us to be sure we cry out to the One who can truly help us.

"Lord, you are with me wherever I am. May I always remember that there is no place where you are not. So when I'm in the depths of my own darkness, I know I can count on you to be there with me. I don't even have to raise my voice. You hear me, and you know what my struggles are and how to help me accept the darkness better than anyone else. May I gradually move into the light with you."

TRUST IN GOD'S GIFTS

I can do all things through him who strengthens me.

—PHILIPPIANS 4:13

One of the most common ways we increase our stress is by failing to trust in our abilities to cope with and address our problems. We undermine ourselves by focusing on our inadequacies and weaknesses and our feelings of helplessness. If we truly want to surrender our stresses and eliminate or weaken their power over us, we can begin by affirming the power we have to cope. God is within us, giving us the strength we need at every moment. Tap into it! Claim it as it was meant to be claimed!

"God of power and might, I call on you to strengthen me as I struggle to cope with my stresses and difficulties. You have given me all that I need to handle these challenges. You will never go back on your word. I trust you, and I also trust myself through the support and power you have placed in me. I am strengthened by you and your presence. With you and your promise of strength, I can do all that I need to do to manage the problems in my life."

Be Present to the Lord

Then I said, "Here I am . . ."

—Psalm 40:7

We try to live a good life, following what we think is our own sacred journey. Yet at times traveling along the road that we think is God's will for us can wind up being difficult. The path that had been smooth and clear can quickly become rocky terrain, filled with puddles and potholes. We don't know which way to go, and we feel frustrated and stressed. In such times, we can ask ourselves these challenging questions: Am I willing to handle and cope with whatever comes along in my life? Do I trust in the Lord enough to say to him, "Here I am"?

"In all the circumstances and events of my life, help me, Lord, to know that no matter what, your love always surrounds me. I want to make a real act of trust in you. Make me strong and trusting enough to simply say, 'Here I am.' Help me to let you call the shots without my direction. You are holding me in your hands, asking for me to do my part, even when it isn't clear what that is. So with all my heart, my God, I say to you: 'Here I am.' Help me to be all and do all that you are asking of me in this situation. You know what's best for me. Whatever you want from me, may I do it well. I count on your direction and help. Here I am."

Surrender in Prayer

"Whatever you ask for in prayer with faith, you will receive."
—Matthew 21:22

Stress can grasp us with such a powerful grip that we feel helpless in getting free. On our own we feel caught, unable to change our experience. That's when we must remind ourselves that we have powerful assistance available to us. Prayer is a way of changing our way of thinking as well as calling for God's help in our struggle. Even asking for help begins to turn our experience in a more positive direction. Believing that we will receive help is a wonderful expression of faith. So what we find is that help comes from two directions: from God's response to our prayer as well as from our own willingness to change our attitudes and thoughts.

"This is a joint endeavor, dear God. I'm calling on you to help me with your powerful love to surrender my stress, which keeps me so caught in its grip. I trust that you will help me. And I see that I must do my part too. By my willingness to ask for your help, I want you to know that I'm serious about letting go of my stress. I've always taken my stress as a given, and then I've just settled down and lived with it. But now I've decided to turn to you. Help me trust in you and your power to support me in releasing this stress in my life."

BREATHE GOD'S LOVE

The spirit of God has made me,
and the breath of the Almighty gives me life.

—JOB 33:4

When we're in distress or upset in any way, it's common for our breathing to become shallow and rapid. Yet it's the very air around us that can bring us to a place of calm and peace. We nourish ourselves with life-giving air when we slow down our breathing and consciously calm ourselves by inhaling and exhaling more deeply.

"O God, who is the very life of my life, you breathe me into existence with every breath I take. Renew my being. Fill me with yourself. With each inhalation, help me to welcome your serenity and peace. With each exhalation, help me to release all the worry, anxiety, and distress that I feel. I give these feelings to you. Renew and refresh me with new life. May I always be conscious of your peace within me."

Be a Child in God's Arms

It was I who taught Ephraim to walk,
I who took them in my arms . . .
And led them with bonds of love.
that I lifted them like a little child to my cheek,
that I bent down to feed them.

—Hosea 11:3-4, REB

No matter how old we are, deep within us we're often aware of a sense of our littleness, our helplessness, and our neediness. Images of ourselves being held close, receiving food, or holding on to someone as we learn to walk can touch our hearts. With a God who picks us up and snuggles us to his cheek in loving warmth, we know we're wrapped in love. How can we be "stressed out" and anxious when we remind ourselves of such care?

"Loving God, the next time that I feel alone and embattled, let me remember these words of Scripture. Let me see and feel my cheek being held close to yours and my whole self being held tenderly in your embrace. Let the feeling of our closeness permeate my mind and heart, and let me know that you are never far from me."

Cast Your Burdens on the Lord!

*Cast your burden on the LORD,
and he will sustain you.*

—PSALM 55:22

Sometimes the heaviness of our worry and stress threatens to overwhelm us. We feel pressed into the ground and unable to move. The sheer weight of the burden seems to paralyze us. In just such times as these, we might imagine ourselves summoning all the energy we can gather and handing all our concerns over to our God, who is waiting before us with open arms. In our imagination, we can watch the burdens melt away as God takes them from us and enfolds them in his love.

"God of great power and strength, I know that you have told me to cast my burdens on you. When I make that move on my own part, then you can do your part, and receive what I've unburdened. Help me do the releasing, which requires my own effort, and then let me trust your promise to sustain and support me."

Turn to God Even in Your Anger

If you are angry, do not be led into sin:
do not let sunset find you nursing your anger.

—Ephesians 4:26, REB

Anger is a spontaneous emotion that we often feel when we are helpless or out of control. In such instances, anger flares up in us, and we lash out at others. Holding on to the angry feelings, or reacting to them by attacking whatever or whoever provoked our anger, continues and prolongs the negative situation. But we have a choice in how we respond to our anger. We can acknowledge it, explore why we feel angry and deal with that specific issue, and then consciously surrender it. And when we are unable to handle our anger, we can turn to God, who is always ready to listen to us—even when we're angry.

"Thank you, God, for the gift of my emotions. The pleasant feelings as well as the painful ones tell me so much about myself. May I deal with them well, and may I appreciate their wisdom and gifts. And when feelings arise that could cause harm to myself or others, may I learn to release them to you."

LOOSEN THE BONDS OF SLAVERY

For freedom Christ has set us free. Stand firm, therefore,
and do not submit again to a yoke of slavery.

—GALATIANS 5:1

If we're honest with ourselves, we can all find some way in which we are caught in a type of slavery—even if we don't initially think of it in these terms. We may be enslaved to food, coffee, drugs, shopping, alcohol, busyness, playing the lottery, TV, and a myriad of other things. All of them have power over us, though we pride ourselves on being "free." To choose to relinquish any of these enslavements would mean freeing ourselves from the huge amount of stress they induce in us. Freeing ourselves from their clutches would also erase some of the emotional worry and distress that we carry in our lives.

"Lord, if I'm going to be enslaved to anything, let it be to you. I want to be your servant, doing the work you call me to do in the world today, whether that be helping the poor, caring for my family, or assisting in my parish. With my cooperation, I ask you to be with me and set me free from anything that might hinder me from serving you with my whole heart."

The Power of Prayer

The prayer of the righteous is powerful and effective.

—James 5:16

So often we feel helpless and ineffective when we don't know how to help a friend or acquaintance in need. We see the pain, sorrow, or distress of another and have a real urge to "fix it" or to take away the suffering. Being willing and available to talk about problems or offer suggestions may be exactly what a person needs.

Many circumstances exist, however, that don't allow for such intimacy. In those situations, let's not forget the silent and powerful help we can give through prayer. Many a person has found comfort and help through the prayers of others they don't even know. What a wonderful way to connect with our brothers and sisters in their times of need! Our prayers can make a powerful contribution.

"Dear God, when I become aware of people around me contending with difficulties in their lives, remind me to pray for them. Let me hold them up to you for healing and comfort or whatever you know is their biggest need. Help them to surrender the stressful situations in their lives to you. Add my care and compassion for them to yours."

REJOICE IN GOD'S FAVOR

"Jesus, Son of David, have mercy on me!"

—MARK 10:47

Every one of us yearns for and has need of compassion and kindness. We plead with God to "let us off the hook," to forgive us, to notice how much we need to be treated with mercy. We can never be all that we would like to be. But because of Jesus' death and resurrection, we can cry out to God to shower us with his mercy. And because of his great love for us, we believe and trust that he hears us and responds. God's loving compassion is always ours. So like Bartimaeus, we must never hesitate to cry out and ask.

"God of great mercy and compassion, here I stand in overwhelming need of you. I open my arms and my heart. Forgive me, and fill me with your mercy and care. Your son, Jesus, told us to ask and receive. So, Father, I do ask: Pour out your mercy on me! Only you know how much I need you and want all that you desire for me. Thank you for giving us your Son. Through him we know that we can always enjoy your mercy, your closeness, and your care."

PRAY YOUR EXPERIENCES

We also boast in our sufferings, knowing that suffering produces
endurance, and endurance produces character,
and character produces hope.

—ROMANS 5:3-4

One of the things we tend to forget (or maybe don't really want to remember) is that our growth takes place through all of our experiences in life. It's often in the difficult struggles—those tough times that feel as if they will do us in—that we grow in courage, strength, or character. Rather than run from our hard times, perhaps we might give some thought to what we could learn from and through them. We might ask God what he wants to teach us through our experiences.

"God of power and might, give me the courage and strength to learn what I need to learn from all the struggles of my life. Hold me and guide me as I learn from them. Teach me and show me the way. I know that you will never abandon me or leave me alone. As I move through my life, may I continue to know that my hope and trust in you will never go unrewarded. I choose to work through my struggles and know that you will be the foundation of my endurance, strength, and hope."

Bear with One Another

Bear with one another and, if anyone has a complaint against another, forgive each other.

—Colossians 3:13

We have the ability to hurt one another. Often we make choices that are hurtful to another person, and they to us. Sometimes we wind up on the inflicting side and sometimes on the receiving side. Interestingly, no matter which side we're on, we suffer. But forgiveness brings healing. Consequently, when someone has treated us poorly or has hurt us in word or in the way they have behaved toward us, we can begin the healing process by being willing to forgive. Healing for both sides can come only when we are each willing to forgive and accept forgiveness.

"Jesus, in the most painful time of your life on earth, as you were receiving both physical and verbal assaults, though you deserved none of it, you showed us how to behave. Your words were clear: 'Father, forgive them, for they do not know what they are doing' (Luke 23:34). Help me choose to be forgiving in my own life. Help me see that when I hold onto my anger and choose to be revengeful, I hurt myself as much as I hurt the other person. No matter how the other person has behaved toward me, I am responsible for what I do or say to them. May I always choose to be loving and forgiving."

Do Not Be Afraid

But when the disciples saw him walking on the sea,
they were terrified, saying, "It is a ghost!" And they cried out in
fear. But immediately Jesus spoke to them and said,
"Take heart, it is I; do not be afraid."

—Matthew 14:26-27

Fear plays a big role in all of our lives. Some of the greatest stresses we experience are caused by the insecurities we face in life and the fear that results, both consciously and unconsciously. Perhaps this story of Jesus walking on the water can speak to us when we feel frightened. Knowing that God is with us in our fears, telling us to "take heart," can be a profound support.

"In any of my stresses and fears, when I feel frightened and worried, Jesus, help me to remember that you are present there. Let me hear you say to me, 'Take heart! Do not be afraid.' If I can believe that you are with me when I'm feeling afraid and stressed, then I will not fear the 'ghosts' that tend to haunt me in these times. I count on you to guide me to those who can support and help me in my distress."

Rejoice in Your Gifts

Do not neglect the gift that is in you.

—1 Timothy 4:14

One common way we tend to operate when we're upset is to generalize our distress to our whole lives. Instead of articulating the specific areas or issues disturbing us, we let them permeate everything. We read our whole life as in trouble rather than naming the particular problem. We also fail to take note of the positive qualities and strengths that we have within us. So when we are struggling with issues that are problematic, perhaps we can move toward healing by clearly naming the specific issues attacking us. At the same time, let's also name the specific strengths and help we have that support us.

"Lord, my refuge and stronghold, help me with this problem. As I make some practical attempts to resolve my difficulties (name the parts to the problem), I also know that I have you at my side, guiding me along my way. I offer you all my weaknesses and needs, trusting you to help me become strong. Help me to recognize the gifts that you have already given me. I thank you for the ways you have already begun to bring me through my distress. You already live within me and know my problems better than I do. I count on your direction, support, and care for me."

CRY OUT TO GOD

O LORD, God of my salvation,
  when, at night, I cry out in your presence,
let my prayer come before you;
  incline your ear to my cry.
For my soul is full of troubles.

—PSALM 88:1-3

Nighttime is when the worries of our lives seem to grow in strength and beg for attention, and we have the feeling that things are out of control. The darkness adds to our sense of helplessness and to the feeling of being lost and not able to see or find our way. Great mystics have spoken of the "dark night of the soul," when they felt lost, alone, and abandoned by God. Perhaps this is the time when we need most to strengthen our trust in God's presence. In the darkness, we can avoid the distractions of the day as we abide with God and ask him to hear our prayers.

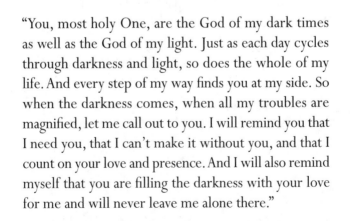

"You, most holy One, are the God of my dark times as well as the God of my light. Just as each day cycles through darkness and light, so does the whole of my life. And every step of my way finds you at my side. So when the darkness comes, when all my troubles are magnified, let me call out to you. I will remind you that I need you, that I can't make it without you, and that I count on your love and presence. And I will also remind myself that you are filling the darkness with your love for me and will never leave me alone there."

THE INTENTION TO DO GOOD

Let all things be done for building up.

—1 CORINTHIANS 14:26

Intention is a very important part of a healthy and fruitful life. Our intention helps us clarify the outcome we want from any of our behaviors and decisions. When we clearly intend something, we begin moving in that direction—even unconsciously—instead of simply taking whatever comes. We've learned over time that our negative expectations may bring us just exactly what we feared. So by actively and creatively coming up with expectations and intentions, and articulating them clearly, we can set ourselves in motion for "building up" rather than breaking down, however that might play out in our lives. May we be creative agents bringing life and growth to ourselves and those around us.

"Creator God, help me to set my intention for this day. May I be an agent of blessing and growth, for myself and for those all around me, even the people I don't know. In all that I do, may I choose a positive, helpful, and loving attitude. Help me to build up, not tear down, all that is good. May I be at peace within myself, and may all my decisions contribute to the well-being of your creation."

Hide in the Lord

You are a hiding place for me;
you preserve me from trouble.

—Psalm 32:7

Sometimes we need to physically remove ourselves from the sources of our stress. When we stay right in the middle of what gets us into trouble, we can make it more difficult for ourselves or others. We know that there are places that nurture us and support our search for peace. So it may be very helpful to create or discover a spot where we can go to collect our thoughts or summon our courage. We can make it a place of prayer, a place to which we retreat when we need a boost or respite. We should use that spot whenever we need it. In that place, we can call upon the presence of God and know that we will be loved and supported.

"O holy One, you love me beyond my wildest dreams. I come to this special place where you are waiting for me, and I sit here with you. You and I have chosen this place—a place where I know I will always be able to find you. I breathe in your warmth and your Spirit. Wherever I am, you are always concerned for me, and you are always with me; but in this place, we are together in a very conscious way. It is here that I can talk to you—about my delight in you and also about what is troubling me. Just by my telling you of my problems, I often discover the answers, which I know come from you. Let this place be blessed, and let me be blessed by our encounter."

Claim Victory in the Lord

I was pushed hard, so that I was falling,
but the Lord helped me.

—Psalm 118:13

Life pushes us hard in many ways, and we see this truth reflected everywhere. Heavy rains flatten fragile new plants against the ground, and ferocious tornado winds rip buildings apart. Aging, accidents, and illnesses cause our vulnerability to surface and our frailty to become all too apparent. Friends and relatives move out of our lives, whether by simple choice, the transience of our society, disagreements, or death, and we feel deeply alone. All of life is marked by the pains and scars of difficulties, losses, and death. Some of these experiences are our greatest challenges and provoke in us the highest levels of stress. We are "pushed hard" and struggle to stay afloat. And yet, the psalmist expresses his victory in the Lord, who helped him when he was falling, and will help us as well.

"Great God of creation, whose design of life includes dying and rising over and over again, be with me in all my deaths, and lead me to the new births that follow them. Even when life pushes me hard, I know that you are alive in me and will stand by me. I can always lean on you when I need support. When I am close to you, even when I am battered by life, I am safe. I trust in you."

Praise the Lord with Every Breath

Let everything that breathes praise the Lord!

—Psalm 150:6

Nature illustrates the harmony of life in this world. For example, trees provide us with oxygen to sustain our lives while we provide them with the carbon dioxide they need. Bees get nectar and pollen from flowers, and by doing so, pollinate the plants. Perhaps we can take a cue from such examples. We can live cooperatively rather than in competition with others. We diminish our stresses when we give of ourselves to others and receive from them what we need.

"Help me to be open and to recognize how healing is this world in which I live, dear God of all creation. May I appreciate the natural world you've given me as my home. May I be grateful for the gift of being part of the workings of the earth. Please help me release my stresses as I rest in the comfort of the world around me. Fill all of creation, and especially me, with praise of you."

Discover God's Gifts in Life

I am the Lord your God,
who teaches you for your own good,
who leads you in the way you should go.
—Isaiah 48:17

It's been said that life is for learning. We're meant to discover the gifts of new life, growth, and learning, even in the midst of all the stresses and strains of our lives. In fact, these are exactly the places where new life is offering itself to us. Every difficult situation—usually a loss of some kind—is a potential birthing ground for new life. We might look at these situations as opportunities to reach that fullness of being that God intended for us. With God's assistance, we may be able to see why these hard times are the "way we should go."

"Gracious God, you continually offer me the opportunity to be born again through all the difficult places in my life. Lead me and guide me in those places. I want to learn and grow through life and become all that you want me to be. Walk with me on my journey, and help me recognize all the birthing places waiting for me."

SEE WITH GOD'S EYES

"Truly I tell you, just as you did it to one of the least of these who are members of my family, you did it to me."

—MATTHEW 25:40

Often our worries and stresses arise from or overflow into our relationships and dealings with other people, provoking turmoil and upset. We offend others and find ourselves feeling offended. We lash out at others and place blame on their shoulders. Maybe we could stop—even right in the middle of the fray—and ask ourselves, "Who is this person in God's eyes?" Would we be able to keep on arguing if we answered, "He or she is a member of God's family, here to care for me, to love me, just as I need to care for him or her"? Many disagreements and quarrels would come to an end if we really believed this truth.

❧

"My loving God, you make very clear what you ask of us. Even the 'least' of the people around me are here as members of your family. Whether they challenge me or comfort me, help me to love them all. I would release loads of stress if I took you at your word and made love the currency of my interactions with everyone. There is no other way I could act if I acknowledged myself and others as united in your Son, Jesus, and members of your family."

The Spirit at Work in You

In each of us the Spirit is seen to be at work
for some useful purpose.

—1 Corinthians 12:7, REB

What a reminder for us when we're feeling down and distressed about life: that through the Spirit in us, each of us has something to offer to this world! And since each of us is a unique being, our gifts cannot be given by others. If we refuse to give to the world what God wants us to give, our special gift will be absent. We must allow God to "wear our faces."

"Here I am, God. You have chosen me to be in a place where you will manifest your Spirit through me. Such a privilege is almost more than I can believe or imagine, and yet I know it to be true. I want to be very aware that I am your ambassador to all the people I meet and relate with today. Help me treasure the fact that you are wearing my face and using my words, hands, and activities to be present to others. O, may I do it well! May you be so pleased that you chose me!"

Cast Your Anxiety on God

Cast all your anxiety on him, because he cares for you.

—1 Peter 5:7

So often we feel heavily burdened by the pressures of our lives. No one else seems to understand, and most folks simply tell us not to worry—which convinces us that they really don't understand. But here's Peter, telling us that all those anxieties we struggle with can be handed over to God, because God does understand and does care for us, and wants to support us and help us with our struggles. Many times just knowing that someone else understands what we're fretting about can be enough to ease the load.

"Here are my anxieties, my God who cares for me. I list them for you, one by one. Just naming them changes the way I feel and gives me a renewed perspective. I place each one of my cares into your hands, and I trust that you will help me deal with them. As I list my anxieties, I realize that I'm making more out of some of them than I need to, so I totally turn them over to you. Other problems may need more attention, and talking with you may help me have new insights about how to handle them. It truly helps to know that my problems are yours as well. Don't let me try to handle them alone. Thank you for caring about me."

CHOOSE CHRIST'S PEACE

Let the peace of Christ rule in your hearts.

—COLOSSIANS 3:15

Every morning when we rise to begin a new day, we make a choice about how we will approach that day. We decide then, even when we're not very aware of it, whether we are going to be looking for trouble or delight. Are we going to face the day with a smiling attitude or with grouchiness and bitterness? The fact is that whatever we've chosen, whether we're aware of it or not, colors everything we do—for us and for everyone around us. What if we made this choice more consciously every morning and said to ourselves, "This is a day I've never seen before and will never see again. I choose to live it with peace in my heart and with gratitude for all the ways I've been blessed"? What a difference such a decision could make!

"God of peace, help me choose to contribute today to the peace of the world. Help me bring an attitude of gratefulness for life and for this day. Show me all the ways I can add to the beauty of the world. Help me choose the peace of Christ for my own heart, because unless I make that choice, I'll never be able to help the world find peace."

Faithful Friends Are a Gift of God

Faithful friends are a sturdy shelter:
whoever finds one has found a treasure.
Faithful friends are beyond price;
no amount can balance their worth.

—Sirach 6:14-15

What a strong and supportive influence good friends can have on us! On the other hand, we can be led in very unhealthy directions by friends who influence us in destructive ways. Many times our choice of "friends" has led us into situations that we know are not good places to be. A desire to surrender our stresses may call for a surrender of those people in our lives who are not really our friends. That may also encourage us to examine ourselves and determine what kind of friend we are to others.

"God, my best and most supportive friend, help me to choose well the people with whom I share time and interests. I know in my heart those who are true friends to me and those who are not. May I let go of those friendships that are influencing me in a negative way. I ask that you watch over these people and help them to become healthier and grow closer to you. I thank you for true friends who support and encourage me as we journey the road of life together. May I also be a true friend to each one of them."

LOVE BANISHES FEAR

In love there is no room for fear; indeed, perfect love banishes fear.
—1 JOHN 4:18, REB

Healthy fear can play a strong and helpful role in our lives, directing us to avoid or steer clear of situations or persons who may be harmful to us. Unhealthy fear can paralyze us and contribute to a sense of wariness and stress in our everyday lives. Often we don't discriminate between these different fears—the healthy and helpful and the unhealthy and harmful. Healthy fear can help us make our way through potentially dangerous situations that we face. Unhealthy fear becomes an enemy in itself, keeping us caught in its clutches and unable to move forward.

"Dear God of wisdom and truth, help me to profit from the healthy and genuine fears that arise in my life. Let their very presence be a source of wisdom for me, helping me find the direction of my growth. Help me discern those fears that paralyze and attempt to cripple me on my journey. May I also learn from them. Rather than allowing these unhealthy fears to overwhelm and entrap me, help me find the message of growth that they hold for me."

Let the Shining Face of God Warm You

May the LORD bless you and guard you;
May the LORD make his face shine on you and
*   be gracious to you;*
May the LORD look kindly on you and give
*   you peace.*

—Numbers 6:24-26, REB

We can all feel the power and radiance contained in this most touching blessing in the Scriptures. Such a collection of images here will surely comfort, heal, protect, and bless anyone in distress who prays these words from the heart. Benevolence permeates this blessing, and we can count on the shining face of God to warm our hearts and clear our minds.

In your imagination, picture the radiant face of God, looking directly at your face with love and kindness. Feel his shining warmth filling your body and sinking into your very bones. Then with great peace say, "Great God of light and warmth, bless me through and through. Look kindly on me, and give me your peace."

Come Away and Rest a While

He said to them, "Come away to a deserted place
all by yourselves and rest a while."

—Mark 6:31

Sometimes when we are in the midst of coping with our stress, we fail to take the time to really assess our lives. We need to step back from our daily habits and routines so that we can be introspective. Then we can begin to figure out whether some of the ways we structure our lives might be setting ourselves up for stress. We can reflect on what our stresses are all about, what brings them on, how they might give us an excuse for avoidance, and what we might be learning from them. By doing so, we may be able to turn them into opportunities for growth.

"Help me come to see how much I choose stress for myself, dear God, and how I might be setting myself up for or even creating the stressors myself. Maybe I'll see how often I am bothered by the same things in my life, and yet keep creating the same circumstances, thoughts, or situations that bring them about. Wake me up to the ways I might be undermining my own life or sabotaging myself."

Be Strong and Courageous

"I hereby command you: Be strong and courageous;
do not be frightened or dismayed, for the LORD your
God is with you wherever you go."

—JOSHUA 1:9

What a powerful statement God spoke to Joshua, and so to us! This isn't a mere suggestion like "Maybe if you could be a little more courageous, you'll get by." Rather, here is a straightforward and clear message: "I command you! Be strong and courageous" in all that you know is right. It is possible for us to develop a resistance to the ill effects of stress, but we need strength and courage as we make the conscious effort to learn how to cope with our challenges in healthy and godly ways.

"God of power and might, you don't expect of me anything more than I have the power to deliver. I rely on your power. Help me stay in touch with your strength and courage, as well as with my own. Help me come to see that you are the one bolstering my trembling knees when I need to stand tall. In hard times, let me surrender my fear and timidity and reach out to grab the sureness of your hand as I learn to cope with my stress."

Let God's Love Be Your Comfort

*Let your steadfast love become my comfort
according to your promise.*

—Psalm 119:76

We look for comfort in so many places. But in the middle of life's difficulties and sorrows, comfort so often eludes us. That's often because we are searching in places that offer superficial, short-lived, or even false comfort—perhaps from people who do not have our best interests at heart or in habits that are addicting. We remember St. Augustine's famous words: "You have made us for yourself, O God, and our hearts are restless until they rest in you." Perhaps we need to look more deeply into the very center of our beings to find comfort in the place where you dwell.

"Help me to still myself, O God, so that I may know your quiet and comforting presence within me. Help me to let go of the places I seek for comfort that always disappoint me. With your care for me and your closeness to me, help me to surrender my grasping at what gives no comfort, and give myself over to your care."

GIVE THE GIFT OF PEACE

*Grace to you and peace from God our Father
and the Lord Jesus Christ.*

—1 CORINTHIANS 1:3

Wouldn't it be wonderful if we could wrap up a package of peace and give it to a friend, family member, or anyone else who is in distress? When they opened our gift, what a profound sense of peace would permeate their minds and bodies! The amazing reality is that we do have the ability to give a gift of peace to each other. The peace we give is that which we carry inside ourselves. Flowing from our relationship with God and from his life within us, this gift comes across in our manner, spirit, and way of being with each other—in what we say and how we act. We know people who have the ability to share their peaceful spirit with others. Much of who we are is communicated in the way we relate to others. Let's look at ourselves and discover how we can give the gift of peace.

"Holy God of peace and grace, of love and care, help me to be a conduit of these same wonderful gifts to others. Help me first be aware of them and open myself to them, and then give these qualities a home in my own heart. May I be fertile soil so that they can grow and flourish within me. Then I will find myself in the blessed position of being able to share these gifts with people who are hungry for them."

WELCOME GOD'S CARE

When anxious thoughts filled my heart,
your comfort brought me joy.

—PSALM 94:19, REB

So often our thoughts determine the mood of our days, coloring and even creating the experiences of our lives. We often don't recognize that we can make a choice to bring more positive thoughts into our minds, and that when we choose other ways of thinking, we'll change the way we feel.

So perhaps when we find ourselves laden with anxieties and worries, we can try replacing our heavy thoughts with lighter and more uplifting ones. We can bring to our minds the thought and image of God's care for us. We might imagine ourselves being comforted by God and held close. As we consciously and deliberately choose images and thoughts of comfort and joy, we will find sadness or anxiety giving way to joy and optimism.

"O God who loves me, help me when I find myself in low or sad places to let go of my painful worries and anxieties. Help me so I don't wallow in them or continue to fret and be anxious, but instead deal with them in practical ways. I know that where you are, joy is. So help me to remind myself that you are with me, and to find the joy and comfort that you bring."

Love without Exception

"You have heard that it was said, 'You shall love your
neighbor and hate your enemy.' But I say to you,
Love your enemies and pray for those who persecute you."
—Matthew 5:43-44

We have great power in our interactions with each other—power that can go in healthy and life-giving directions or that can be hurtful and destructive. Amazingly, both parties are affected by how we each choose to deal with the other—it never goes just one way. When we choose (and "choose" is the significant word) to be loving rather than hateful, even if we find the other person's behavior negative and difficult, we may find that we've lowered the stress level in ourselves and sown love and peace around us.

"God, help me learn that I can be loving in every situation. It may not be my spontaneous reaction, especially when someone is hurtful and I feel inclined to be hurtful in response. But help me respond with love rather than react with anger. Help me know that I have a choice to make—that no one else's behavior can force me to respond in one particular way. I can choose what I want my response to be. Then, when I choose to be loving, I'll discover that the stress-inducing emotions of anger and revenge give way to a greater peacefulness in me, which may well sow seeds of love and peace in the other person too."

ALL THINGS WORK TOGETHER FOR GOOD

We know that all things work together
for good for those who love God.

—ROMANS 8:28

When we are feeling particularly burdened and stressed, it's easy to lose hope and forget the truth of this Scripture verse. St. Paul asserts that for those who love God, *all* things "work together for good." If we look back over our lives, we can see that there have been times when good things unexpectedly emerged from the very ground of troubles and struggles. Unbeknownst to us, our trials provided the soil and fertilizer for our growth and learning.

"As I purposefully look at the struggles in my life, my God, may I find a surprise there—as unlikely as that seems to me. I know that some aspect of my difficulties could be the very place where you are showing or teaching me something I need to learn. God, maybe if I make the decision to learn the lesson, I'll find that with your help, something new is coming out of the problem places of my life. Nourish my growth in those places, and open my eyes to the potential gifts there."

Be Peaceful and Gentle

Keep alert, stand firm in your faith, be courageous,
be strong. Let all that you do be done in love.

—1 Corinthians 16:13-14

Being peaceful and gentle, qualities that help us in our journey through life, are not contradictory to firmness, courage, or strength, nor do they prevent us from being loving. When we are strong and firm in our beliefs, we are able to say no to those choices before us that can increase our stress. Sometimes we need the courage to change stress-inducing situations or unhealthy ways of relating to others. We can stand firm against circumstances that are detrimental to our health and spiritual well-being. As we stay firm and strong in the Lord, we can allow the Spirit to steer us in growth-filled directions that reduce our anxieties and help us manage our stresses.

"God, I see that you are not asking anything of me that doesn't contribute to my growth and to my becoming a whole, healthy, holy person in this world. To be strong, to be firm in my faith, to be peaceful and loving—in all these ways my life will give you glory. So please, guide me to make good choices and decisions. Help me know when to say no and when to say yes. Help me to trust your presence within me—loving me, bringing me peace, and showing me how I can contribute to the peace and love of the world."

Peace Be to You

The LORD said to him, "Peace be to you; do not fear."
—JUDGES 6:23

Fear lies behind much of our stress. We expend so much energy worrying and being anxious about countless issues in our lives. We lie awake at night, our minds running through a list of what might or might not happen. We are anxious about how we might not measure up to what life asks of us. We fret over the possible outcomes of problems in our lives. We spend most of our time focused on the future, and almost totally avoid living in the present as we stew and fret about all the "what if's." Consequently, we miss God in the only place God lives—the present moment.

"God of peace, I know you are here with me and that you also know all my worries. Remind me always that I haven't been able to come up with any worries and concerns that aren't already in your hands. When I find myself becoming fearful, help me to stop and recall your presence within me. You bring peace to my life, and I need to open myself to it by surrendering to you all those fears and worries that fill my mind."

Let Silence Speak Peace

The Lord is in his holy temple;
let all the earth keep silence before him!

—Habakkuk 2:20

Noise often bombards us from every direction, preventing us from hearing anything else. We hear the sounds of traffic or the hum of a fan, which become "white noise" that we barely notice. We say to ourselves, "I can't hear myself think," yet we often add to the din with the blare of our television and radios. Sometimes it's only in a more natural setting, perhaps outdoors in the woods, that we can get away from electronic devices and traffic, and find any degree of quiet. Yet only we can make the decision to go to a quiet place—that still point deep down within each of us—where God is. It is a place untouched by stress.

I breathe deeply and relax with each exhalation. Gradually I move beyond sound and into that quiet place. With each breath I move more and more into peaceful quiet. I begin to release the chatter in my mind. If I want to be at peace and speak God's language of love, I move away from words. As I feel the breath entering my body and then being released, I know that God is breathing within me, each breath sustaining my life. I let our connection in this silent place be my profound prayer.

Return a Blessing

Finally, all of you, have unity of spirit, sympathy, love for one another, a tender heart, and a humble mind. Do not repay evil for evil or abuse for abuse; but, on the contrary, repay with a blessing.

—1 Peter 3:8-9

What a gift to the world it would be if each of us agreed to these directives—if we could say that these are the requirements for being members of the human family. So often we readily defend ourselves when someone offends us, and we wind up repaying that offense by being offensive ourselves. How the experience would change on both sides if we returned a blessing to the other person and broke the pattern of repaying abuse with more abuse. Not only would we stand on the side of blessing, but we would be more likely to elicit a blessing from the other person. The stress of such painful interactions would be relieved.

"God, this is my prayer today:
Give me a tender heart, a heart that is able to be moved. Give me a sympathetic spirit, a spirit that feels the pain of others. Give me a humble mind, a mind that sees no on as inferior or superior. Give me an awareness of the common spirit that we all share. Help me to be loving to every one, as you are, my God. And help me to see that you can use me to pour blessings on all who cross my path by the way I deal with them. May we all share in the blessing. Amen."

AGREE WITH GOD

"Agree with God, and be at peace;
in this way good will come to you."

—JOB 22:21

According to this Scripture verse, the key to achieving peace is to "agree with God." But what does that mean? The dictionary says that to agree means "to be of one mind" or to be "in harmony with." Apparently, this isn't the way we usually live, since Scripture also has God saying, "Your ways are not my ways" and "your thoughts are not my thoughts" (see Isaiah 55:8). The challenge for us is to take a fresh look at our own thoughts and ways of being. As we reexamine them, we may find that our thoughts and habits are not always in agreement with God's. If we are honest with ourselves, we will probably discover areas in our lives where we could align ourselves more readily with what we know are God's ways.

"Loving God, if there's a difference between how I look at something and how you look at the same thing, I know that your way is the way I need to go. When I look at things differently, it may be that I'm just fooling myself because I'd rather have what I want instead of what I know is your will. Please help me begin by being honest with myself, so that you and I will wind up on the same page. I want to be in harmony with you. Give me eyes and a heart to see how much you want me aligned with you, and forgive me for the times I've strayed."

Rejoice in God's Presence

Seek the Lord and his strength,
seek his presence continually.

—1 Chronicles 16:11

We seem to believe that we must look for God, that we must search to find our God. Yet all the while, what we really need to realize is that God is not lost or hiding from us, but with us in this very moment. We're the ones who get lost and forget that we are forever in the presence of God! All we need to do is remind ourselves of this truth. Now is the only time we ever have. This present moment is the place where I am and where God is, because Christ lives in me. Maybe I can challenge myself to become alert to God's movements, right now, in my life and in my heart.

"I ask you to be here with me, God, and then I remember that you *are* already here with me. My hope is that I may be here with you. I know you are ever present and that my job is simply to wake up to that reality. I know that you are with me whether I am managing my stress well or whether it is getting me down. Help me choose to bring myself back to the present moment and notice the opportunities that you are holding out to me. I want to seek you continuously."

Find God Within

How long, O Lord? Will you forget me forever?
How long will you hide your face from me?

—Psalm 13:1

In the bustle of our daily lives, as we multitask and run in circles, trying to do all that we believe is necessary, we may develop a sense of being lost in the process. We may feel that God has found no space to fit into our lives, and so has moved away. These are the times we want to make a special effort to find God within us. Let us choose to make that space by taking five minutes, or even just two minutes, to quiet ourselves and turn to God. Since listening is also a major part of any conversation, as we talk to our Lord, we may want to listen to what he wants to say to us. Do we open ourselves to hear what God may be telling us?

"Heavenly Father, it's more likely that I've forgotten you than that you've forgotten me. Your face may be hidden from me because I've forgotten to look for you. I know that you are closer to me than I am to myself, as you are in everyone. Challenge me to find you in places and people all around me—specific ones at each moment. Help me hear your voice saying to me, 'Can you see me here?'"

BE CLOTHED IN FAITH AND PEACE

"But if God so clothes the grass of the field, which is alive today and tomorrow is thrown into the oven, how much more will he clothe you—you of little faith!"

—LUKE 12:28

We marvel at the beauty of a hillside covered with an array of spring flowers. Though they may differ in size, shape, and color, each flower uniquely manifests the wonder of its creator. Perhaps we could find the "clothes" in which we are meant to manifest God's beauty—love, joy, peace, kindness, and all those virtues we can make our own. What a fitting way to radiate the wonder of our creator!

"Let my faith and trust in you, God of great beauty, make me strong so that I never doubt that you will always take care of me. Teach me to choose the 'clothes' in which I travel through this world so that they radiate your qualities. Help me to make your qualities my own. Help me to stop worrying about things that have no real significance."

Don't Worry about Tomorrow

"So do not worry about tomorrow, for tomorrow will bring worries of its own. Today's trouble is enough for today."

—Matthew 6:34

We often worry about the future. One worry leads us to another, so we lose sleep, and our stress overflows onto the lives of those around us. Jesus knew all about human nature—after all, he shared it with us. He's saying to us, "There will always be things you can choose to worry about, but focus on today, since today is all you'll ever have." What we worry about for tomorrow may never happen, and our energy is wasted. So Jesus would tell us, "Live in the present! Attend to today and let tomorrow be. And know that I'll still be with you tomorrow, even as I am today."

"Jesus, help me see that all I ever have is right now, the present moment. Help me to cope well with the 'right nows' of my life, and not borrow trouble from the future. Help me so I don't magnify my worries—or turn them into more than they really are. So for today, I name my biggest concerns, one at a time, and give some thought to how I might address them now. Help me do what I can. Then I place them in your hands and let them go."